GET A JOB

AT THE

AIRPORT

JOE RHATIGAN

Created and produced by
Bright Futures Press, Cary, North Carolina
www.brightfuturespress.com

Published by
Cherry Lake Publishing, Ann Arbor, Michigan
www.cherrylakepublishing.com

Photo Credits: cover, Shutterstock/corepics VOF; page 4, Shutterstock/muratart; page 5, Shutterstock/Mario Hagen; page 7, Shutterstock/Monkey Business Images; page 7, Shutterstock/Kasza; page 9, Shutterstock/ssguy; page 11, Shutterstock/Policas; page 11, Shutterstock/Vlad Teedor; page 13, Shutterstock/View Apart; page 15, Shutterstock/Neale Cousland; page 15, Shutterstock/Andresr; page 17, Shutterstock/Kotsovolos Panagiotis; page 19, Shutterstock/Burben; page 19, Shutterstock/Robert Adrian Hillman; page 21, Shutterstock/bikeriderlondon; page 23, Shutterstock/Monika Wisniewska; page 23, Shutterstock/Blend Images; page 25, Shutterstock/StudioSmart; page 26, Shutterstock/hxdbzxy; page 27, Shutterstock/alice-photo; page 28, Shutterstock/Alexander Chaikin.

Illustrated by Chris Griffin

Library of Congress Cataloging-in-Publication Data

Names: Rhatigan, Joe, author.
Title: Get a job at the airport / by Joe Rhatigan.
Description: Ann Arbor, Mich. : Cherry Lake Publishing, 2016. | Series: Get a
    job | Audience: Grade 4 to 6. | Includes index.
Identifiers: LCCN 2016006909| ISBN 9781634719032 (hardcover) | ISBN
    9781634719261 (pdf) | ISBN 9781634719490 (pbk.) | ISBN 9781634719728
    (ebook)
Subjects: LCSH: Airports--Juvenile literature. |
    Airports--Employees--Juvenile literature.
Classification: LCC HE9797 .R43 2016 | DDC 387.7364023--dc23
LC record available at https://lccn.loc.gov/2016006909

Printed in the United States of America

TABLE OF CONTENTS

Going somewhere?

If it's far away, you'll probably take an airplane. Visiting a large airport is a lot like entering a gigantic mall. There are shops everywhere. Escalators and moving sidewalks carry people up and down and back and forth. Small electric cars ferry passengers to their next flight. There are restaurants, televisions, newsstands, and waiting areas. In some airports, there are even train stations. Unless you look out a window, you may actually forget you're at an airport!

It takes a small city of employees to operate the airport. Some of these workers fly the planes. Others help you get your airline tickets. Still others make sure your luggage arrives at the same place you do. And these are only some of the jobs!

To learn more about working at an airport, we're sending the ever curious and often clumsy **J**eremiah **O**liver **B**aumgartner on a family vacation. Everyone calls Jeremiah "Job" because of his initials. Now, Job isn't a real kid, but the kinds of workers he encounters on his trip to the airport are.

This book will give you lots of great information about these jobs. Next time you take off for parts unknown, see how many of these workers you can spot.

FLIGHT FACT

There are more than 600,000 people working in the United States' 13,000 airports.

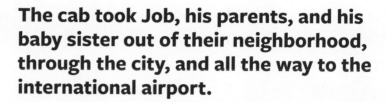

The cab took Job, his parents, and his baby sister out of their neighborhood, through the city, and all the way to the international airport.

Job kept looking up at the sky. Every time he saw an airplane, he imagined himself that far up. It was a little scary, but mostly it was very exciting!

He pointed to a plane and said to his sister, "Look! We will be up there soon! And everyone down here will look smaller than ants."

"Gaaaarp," said his sister.

When the family arrived at the airport, they got out of the cab and walked toward the airport **terminal**. This is the place where passengers get boarding passes, check luggage, and go through security.

Skycaps meet passengers at curbside drop-off points, and help them with heavy luggage and other oversized items. They also get wheelchairs for passengers who need them. Skycaps show passengers where to check in or, in some cases, they check passengers in for their flights right there at the curb.

Airline ticket agents stand behind a counter and greet passengers, take luggage that will be packed in the airplane's cargo **hold** area, and make seat assignments. Ticket agents also help customers make changes to their flight or buy tickets. Agents often have to be patient and kind as they deal with customers angry about sudden changes in the flight schedule or worried about missing their flight.

The luggage you hand to the airline ticket agent is placed on a conveyor belt and disappears through an opening in the back wall. The bags arrive at a bag room where **baggage handlers** take over. Also known as ramp agents, the handlers sort, load, and unload passengers' baggage and other cargo. They use forklifts, baggage tugs, and other vehicles to get the bags to and from an airplane.

Friendly ticket agents help passengers with tickets and baggage.

Screeners, who work for the federal government's **Transportation Security Administration** (TSA), check everyone's identification. Then examine passengers' carry-on bags through x-ray scanners. Screeners also direct passengers to walk through metal detectors or body scanners. What are they looking for? Screeners are looking for items that are not allowed on

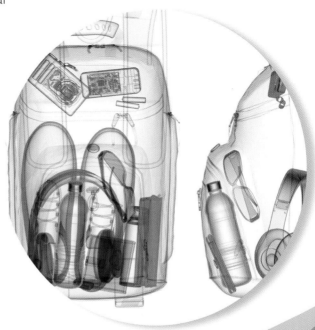

X-ray screeners peek inside carry-on bags.

airplanes such as weapons, dangerous liquids or chemicals, sharp items, and more. It's their job to make sure every flight is as safe as possible.

THE RESULTS

Job was anxious to get to the gate where they would get on their airplane. But first he had to get through the very long security line. "Why do we have to wait in so many lines?" he asked.

His dad answered, "Lots of people want to fly and the airport has to keep people safe."

When it was Job's turn to go through the **security checkpoint**, he took off his shoes and jacket, put his backpack on the conveyor line, and stepped inside the x-ray machine.

Once inside, he raised his arms, while the scanner made a quick circle around his body.

"I wonder if they can see what I ate for breakfast," Job asked.

Job couldn't believe how big the airport actually was.

There were stores, restaurants, newsstands, and yogurt stands. Most of all, there were people everywhere.

Since his flight wasn't supposed to leave for another hour, Job wandered around the terminal. Before he found his way back to his **departure gate**, he got lost twice, tripped over three backpacks, and accidentally unplugged four computer cords.

His mom said, "There are many people who work behind the scenes at the airport."

"I'm glad I don't work at an airport," Job said.

"Why's that?" his mom asked.

"I think I would get lost every morning just trying to find where I'm supposed to be!"

From an office in the terminal building, the **airport manager** works to keep the airport operating safely and efficiently every day. This means following government rules for operating an airport and fixing any problems that come up. The manager works with **vendors** who sell food, airlines that fly planes in and out of the airport, and all the teams needed to manage the airport.

Safety is always on the mind of **airline operations agents**. They patrol and inspect the airfield as well as the terminal for safety hazards and security problems. They check **runways** to make sure all the lights are working and that there is no broken pavement. If birds are on the runway, operations agents chase them away so planes can take off or land. Operations agents stay alert and on the lookout for people who are in places they don't belong.

Airline operations agents make sure runways are clear for takeoff and landing.

A large airport has more than one airline operating planes there. Each airline employs their own people, including an **airline station manager**. This person is in charge of an airline's ground operations, which include ticketing, check-in, baggage, and boarding. The station manager's job makes sure that the airline's flights leave on time with the right people, luggage, and cargo on board.

Hidden somewhere at the airport is the food service center, where cooks, **food preparation agents**, and other kitchen staff prepare meals. They will feed passengers taking long flights or flying **first class**. These employees cook the food and set up the dishes and silverware in

Airline terminals are full of shops and restaurants to serve passengers.

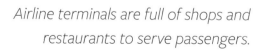

ready-to-eat containers. Other food preparation agents transport the meals from the food service center to the airplanes where the meals will be served during flights.

The **reservation sales agent** gives travel information to an airline's customers either online or over the phone. They may also help with trip planning, renting cars, fare information, meals, and anything else customers need for their flight plans. A customer may also reserve and pay for a flight with the reservation sales agent.

HOLD THAT PLANE!

It's a nice change of pace to see someone *else* in trouble besides me.

THE RESULTS

Job and his father played a game in which they would guess if a person passing by was a passenger or an employee.

"It is easy to tell the difference," Dad explained. "Anyone carrying something—luggage or a backpack—is a passenger. If someone is in a uniform or walking like they're going somewhere important, they work here."

"Got it," Job said, "And if someone is running like crazy, they're probably about to miss their flight!"

CHAPTER 3
JOB TOURS THE TERMINAL

Job was getting dizzy looking at everything the airport had to offer.

So his mom took him over to the wall of windows to watch the planes departing and landing.

"Wow!" Job said. "I didn't even notice this. What are those little people out there doing?"

"The people aren't little," his mom said. "The planes are just that big."

A **ramp marshal** is in charge of directing planes to and from their **hangars**. Ramp marshals use lighted orange wands to signal pilots to turn, slow down, stop, and shut down engines. It's like directing traffic but instead of cars, they direct huge jets.

Equipment drivers operate carts, buses, food and fuel trucks, and the ramp stands and stairways used to get people on and off some airplanes. Drivers are responsible for making sure their equipment is working correctly and getting it fixed if it's not. Drivers must stay alert so they don't mistakenly crash into airplanes or other vehicles.

Fuelers climb onto aircraft wings to fill fuel tanks.

Fuelers drive a truck filled with special aviation fuel to airplanes in need of refueling. The fueler then climbs onto a wing of the aircraft with the fuel hose and fills the tank. They may also help with emptying the airplane's bathroom holding tank, which is done with a **suction** hose from outside the airplane.

The workers with the tools are the **mechanics**. Their duty is to fix problems that develop with airplanes as well as perform many inspections to make sure everything on an airplane is in working order.

Ramp marshals direct planes in and out of departure gates.

FLIGHT FACT
The world's airports service nearly 7 billion passengers a year!

Avionics mechanics are responsible for the aircraft's communications and flight electronics. **Powerplant and airframe mechanics** work on engines, landing gear, and the outside (or hull) of a plane.

The **ground controller** is in charge of making sure all the people, trucks, carts, and planes stay out of each other's way. Ground controllers direct planes between the terminal and the runway and keep them safe distances away from other planes as they taxi (move toward or away from the runway). Ground controllers are in charge of directing airplanes for as long as the plane is on the ground. This job moves on to air traffic control once the plane is in the air.

THE RESULTS

After about 30 minutes of staring out the window, Job got confused. Everything starting blurring together and he could no longer see very clearly. "Is it getting foggy out there?"

"No, Job," his mother said. "You've just fogged up the window by standing with your face so close to it!"

CHAPTER 4
JOB ON BOARD

"What's that tall building over there?" Job asked, pointing towards a large tower from his foggy window.

"That's the air traffic control tower," his mom said. "That's where people and computers help direct planes in the air."

"So it's like the brains of the airport," Job said.

"That's right."

"Well then," Job said, "can someone send a message to the brain that I'm ready to leave now?"

Air traffic controllers use radar, computers, and radios to watch and direct traffic in the sky in order to keep airplanes at a safe distance from each other. The safety of the pilots, crew, and passengers depends on the air traffic controllers, who direct thousands of planes over the course of the day. They tell pilots when to take off and land, what direction to go, and how to avoid bad weather. Needless to say, this is a stressful job.

Considered part of the flight crew, but located in the control tower, a **flight dispatcher** works with a pilot to make sure the flight is safe and on time. To do this, the dispatcher creates a flight plan, which is a schedule of where the plane will land, how long it will stay at each airport, how much distance the plane will travel, how much fuel the plane will need, and how weather may affect the trip. The dispatcher is in charge of specific planes, and keeps track of them on a radar display. Using maps, computers, and weather reports, the dispatcher helps those pilots make good decisions.

Air traffic controllers direct traffic in the sky.

The ever-changing weather can cause problems for flights across the country. **Aviation meteorologists** keep a close eye on the weather and give up-to-date information to pilots and flight dispatchers so they can avoid turbulence due to wind, clouds, rain, or snow. What makes this job more difficult than a regular forecaster's job is that aviation meteorologists have to know the weather at different **altitudes** in the sky. They use radars, computers, and information from weather stations to make accurate forecasts.

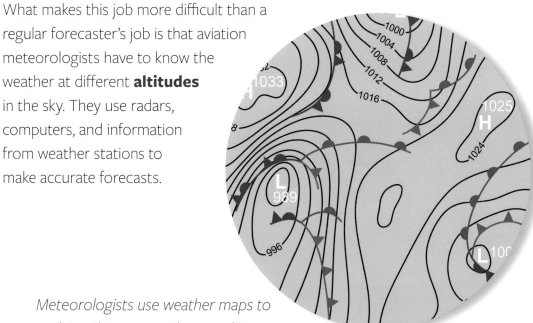

Meteorologists use weather maps to update pilots on weather conditions.

THE RESULTS

Finally, their flight number was called, and Job and his family walked toward the gate that would lead them to their plane.

"Oh, great, another line!" Job said. "If we don't hurry, we're going to have to stand in the aisles like on a train!"

"Don't worry," his mom said. "We have reserved seats."

FLIGHT FACT

There are around 15,000 air traffic controllers working in the United States.

I wonder if those overhead compartments are where they keep the snacks...

Job gave his boarding pass to a man standing by a doorway.

Then he walked down a long hallway that seemed like it would never end. He walked through a door where a nice woman said hello to him.

Job was not sure where he was exactly. So he asked, "Can someone tell me when we'll be on the plane? I've been waiting all day!"

"Um, Job," his dad answered, "you're on the plane now."

"Oh ..."

The man who took Job's boarding pass is called a **station agent**. These agents work at the arrival and departure gates helping passengers board the planes. They also help passengers getting off planes find their next flight, and they make announcements about flights boarding, arriving, and departing.

Pilots fly the plane. The head pilot on a flight is also known as the captain. The pilot makes all the flight decisions once in the air, while communicating with air traffic controllers and the pilots of other aircraft that are nearby. Pilots often make announcements during the flight to reassure passengers about things like arrival times and weather. Pilots are responsible for the safety of the passengers and the crew. They must train for a long time before they can fly aircraft on their own.

The **first officer** is also known as the co-pilot and is second-in-command of the aircraft. The first officer helps the captain fly the craft and will go through the safety checklist with the captain before takeoff. Large aircraft need at least two pilots so that one can fly the plane while the other is monitoring the controls. Really large flights may have second or third officers as well.

Pilots fly planes from the cockpit in the front of an airplane.

The **flight attendants** attend to the passengers on a plane. They focus on safety and comfort, while providing drinks, snacks and meals, and information. Before flights, flight attendants perform safety checks on life vests and other items needed in an emergency, and before takeoff, they do a safety demonstration for passengers. One of the many benefits of being a flight attendant is that you get to travel around the world and do a lot of sightseeing.

Flight attendants take care of passengers' safety and comfort needs.

One person you will not meet on the airplane, but who may be working without you even knowing it, is an **air marshal**. They work for the government, and it's their job to protect passengers and crews on airplanes from dangerous people. Air marshals don't fly on every flight, but they do travel often and are allowed to carry guns on the plane. They are trained to stop people before they can do something illegal or dangerous on an airplane.

I guess I should have paid closer attention when they did the seat belt demonstration.

THE RESULTS

"Finally, we're on the plane and ready to take off," Job said. "It feels like it took all day just to get to my seat."

Job listened to the pilot talk about their flight and then paid close attention as a flight attendant demonstrated proper safety procedures during an emergency. Soon they were in the air, heading way up to their cruising altitude.

Job looked at his baby sister and said, "Isn't this amazing? This is the most exciting day of my life. We are actually FLYING in an airplane!"

"Gaaaarp," his sister replied.

"What's that tall building over there?" Job asked, pointing towards a large tower from his foggy window.

Groan... I think we could have *walked* to Hawaii by now.

"That's the air traffic control tower," his mom said. "That's where people and computers help direct planes in the air."

"So it's like the brains of the airport," Job said.

"That's right."

"Well then," Job said, "can someone send a message to the brain that I'm ready to leave now?"

Air traffic controllers use radar, computers, and radios to watch and direct traffic in the sky in order to keep airplanes at a safe distance from each other. The safety of the pilots, crew, and passengers depends on the air traffic controllers, who direct thousands of planes over the course of the day. They tell pilots when to take off and land, what direction to go, and how to avoid bad weather. Needless to say, this is a stressful job.

Considered part of the flight crew, but located in the control tower, a **flight dispatcher** works with a pilot to make sure the flight is safe and on time. To do this, the dispatcher creates a flight plan, which is a schedule of where the plane will land, how long it will stay at each airport, how much distance the plane will travel, how much fuel the plane will need, and how weather may affect the trip. The dispatcher is in charge of specific planes, and keeps track of them on a radar display. Using maps, computers, and weather reports, the dispatcher helps those pilots make good decisions.

Air traffic controllers direct traffic in the sky.

The ever-changing weather can cause problems for flights across the country. **Aviation meteorologists** keep a close eye on the weather and give up-to-date information to pilots and flight dispatchers so they can avoid turbulence due to wind, clouds, rain, or snow. What makes this job more difficult than a regular forecaster's job is that aviation meteorologists have to know the weather at different **altitudes** in the sky. They use radars, computers, and information from weather stations to make accurate forecasts.

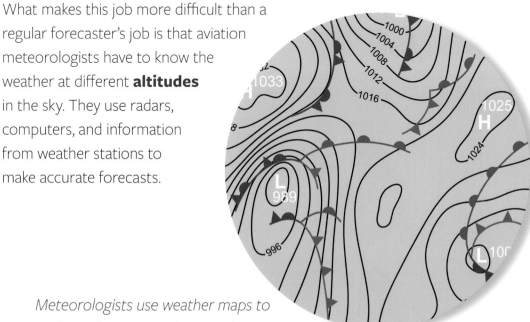

Meteorologists use weather maps to update pilots on weather conditions.

THE RESULTS

Finally, their flight number was called, and Job and his family walked toward the gate that would lead them to their plane.

"Oh, great, another line!" Job said. "If we don't hurry, we're going to have to stand in the aisles like on a train!"

"Don't worry," his mom said. "We have reserved seats."

FLIGHT FACT
There are around 15,000 air traffic controllers working in the United States.

CHAPTER 6

WHO DOES WHAT AT AIRPORTS?

WHO DOES WHAT?

Job met lots of people with interesting jobs at the airport. Can you match their job titles with the correct job description?

Please do NOT write in this book if it is not yours. Use a separate piece of paper.

1. Person who helps passengers plan trips and make reservations by phone or online.

2. Person who sorts, loads, and unloads passengers' luggage onto airplanes.

3. Person who repairs mechanical problems on airplanes.

4. Person who helps pilots make flight plans.

5. Person who takes care of passengers during flights.

A. Flight dispatcher

B. Mechanic

C. Baggage handler

D. Reservation sales agent

E. Flight attendant

Answer Key: 1-D; 2-C; 3-B; 4-A; 5-E

WHO? WHAT? WHERE?

Choose the correct job title to complete the sentences below.

1. A _____ flies an airplane.

2. A _____ prepares meals that are served on long flights or in first class.

3. An _____ directs traffic in the sky.

4. A _____ refuels airplanes in between flights.

5. A _____ makes seat assignments and gives passengers their boarding passes.

A. ticket agent

B. food preparation agent

C. fueler

D. air traffic controller

E. pilot

Hey, Job here! We had a great flight and a wonderful vacation, although my baby sister cried a lot on the flight and everybody stared at us.

Pssst ... If this book doesn't belong to you, write your answers on a separate sheet of paper so you don't get in BIG trouble.

Now that you've read a little about my adventure at an airport, it's your turn. Write a story about a trip (real or imaginary) that you took. Be sure to mention all the people you saw doing different jobs.

Go online to download a free activity sheet at **www.cherrylakepublishing.com/activities.**

GLOSSARY

air marshal
government worker who travels on planes and provides security

air traffic controller
person who directs airplane traffic in the sky

airline operations agent
airport employee who patrols and inspects the airfield and the terminal for safety hazards and security problems

airline station manager
employee in charge of that airline's ground operations, making sure flights leave on time as well as ticketing, check-in, and more

airline ticket agent
airline employee who gives passengers their boarding passes and takes luggage that will be placed in the cargo area of the airplane

airport manager
person in charge of operating an airport

airport station attendant
airport employee who helps passengers inside the terminal and answers questions as needed

altitude
the height of an object or point in relation to sea level or ground level

aviation meteorologist
person who gives up-to-date weather information to flight crews

avionics mechanic
worker responsible for fixing problems with an airplane's electronic systems

baggage handler
worker who sorts and delivers passenger luggage to the correct airplane

departure gate
passageway where passengers embark or disembark from airplanes

equipment driver
airport employee who operates one or more of the many trucks and carts on the ground

first class
the most expensive and most luxurious class of accommodation on an airplane

first officer
the co-pilot and second-in-command of an airplane

flight attendant
airline employee who helps passengers on a plane with safety and comfort

flight dispatcher
airport employee who works with pilots via radio communication to make sure the flight is safe and on time

food preparation agent
member of the kitchen staff who prepares food for the different flights

fueler
worker who fills airplanes with the fuel needed for flight

ground controller
employee who makes sure all the people, trucks, carts, and planes on the ground stay out of each other's way

hangar
a large room or area where aircraft is stored

hold
the part of an airplane where goods are stored

mechanic
worker who fixes problems with airplanes so they can fly safely

pilot
the captain of the plane in charge of flying the craft

powerplant and airframe mechanic
person who fixes engines, landing gear, and the hull of airplanes

ramp marshal
airport employee who directs planes to and from their hangars

reservation sales agent
a customer service specialist who helps callers book flights and plan trips

runway
a leveled strip of smooth ground along which aircraft take off and land

screener
government employee who makes sure passengers are not bringing anything dangerous onto the airplane

security checkpoint
area where passengers and carry-on baggage is screened for safety purposes

skycap
person who helps passengers check their luggage and get their boarding passes

station agent
employee who takes passengers' boarding passes before entering the aircraft

suction
the act of removing air from a space in order to suck materials into an empty space

terminal
the building where passengers first enter when they arrive at the airport

Transportation Security Administration (TSA)
an agency of the U.S. Department of Homeland Security that has authority over the security of the traveling public in the United States

vendors
people who sell things

INDEX

ABOUT THE AUTHOR

Joe Rhatigan is an accident-prone author whose works include *Ouch! The Weird & Wild Ways Your Body Deals with Agonizing Aches, Ferocious Fevers, Lousy Lumps, Crummy Colds, Bothersome Bites, Breaks, Bruises & Burns*; *White House Kids*; and *Inventions That Could Have Changed the World, But Didn't*. He lives in Asheville, North Carolina, with his wife and three kids.